Dishy-Washy

Story by Joy Cowley
Illustrations by Elizabeth Fuller

Mr. Wishy-Washy
washes dishes.
He is the best dishwasher
in the state of Washington.

He washes cups and mugs,
dishy-washy, dishy-washy.

He washes plates and bowls,
dishy-washy, dishy-washy.

He washes pots and pans,
dishy-washy, dishy-washy.

He washes the cat's dish,
dishy-washy, dishy-washy.

He washes the cat.

"Mee-ow!" cries the cat,
and it jumps right out.

Down come the
pots and pans.

Down come the
plates and bowls.

Down come the
cups and mugs.

12

"Oh, my!"
says Mr. Wishy-Washy.

Now, when
Mr. Wishy-Washy
washes dishes,
he watches
what he's washing.

And the cat does, too.

Dishy-washy,
dishy-washy.
Purr, purr, purr.